Hysteria

A Collection of Shivers

Written By

LiAna Maria Rivera

Dedicated to the outcasts, young lovers, and the mad.

Trigger Warnings: This book contains themes of self-harm, violence, attempted suicide, addiction, and other triggers that may be unsuitable for some readers.

Please stop reading here if you are easily triggered by things of this nature.

The Hysteria

The Hysteria is a world that exists closer to reality, but further than most human perception.

Only a few of us reach this state of mind, through our eyes, ears, hands; most never act on it, choosing creativity like me and you.

A place we rest our idle desires, destructive thoughts, and the shadows of ourselves.

When I found this land, everything in it was red, stained with memories better left repressed; forgotten.

This land was riddled with destruction left behind from hurricanes and whirlwinds; uprooted trees, wilting flowers, drowned doves, clouds overcast, poison in the air, and invisible rain that can be felt, but not seen.

If left untreated the Hysteria spreads, deadlier by the second.

The treatment I've chosen is art.

-FEAR-

Fear

A butterfly spreads its wings across my psyche
Sprouted from a centered crevice in my brain.
The sparks of electricity
Shock my motor ability.
And I'm paralyzed.
The darkness stretches near, surrounding me.
I can feel icy cold hands touching me
Before the trance is broken
And my feet move on their own.
Pure instinct carries me
On the feathered wings of survival.
Until I feel a sharp split-second of pain.
Everything goes red before I see lights
And fade away through broken sight.

Shadows

They lurk about in every corner,
And go unnoticed by all others.
Ever so evident yet hidden in plain sight.
While they spoil our necessities of life.
Have you ever seen true evil before?
Oh, my friend, you have been misinformed.
Listen to me now; I'll expose the truth.
These beasts, you see—they seduce!
The strongest of us as they dance away.
In the brightest, lightest, shine of day.
Taunting you, and watching me...
From even the deepest depths of the sea.
These phantoms of darkness loom in the background.
An outlandish mystery, so profound!
The demons that mock us and laugh at our pain,
As we slowly go insane.

Layers

Thinking, thinking, I'm overthinking.
I'm conscious of it, but it's
Overwhelming, overbearing,
I'm overthinking.
"I'm alone, alone
You don't understand!"
Just take my hand...
"No, no, it's too much to ask!"
Think about what you're doing—
"That's right, I am."
Overthinking!
Do it, go on, don't listen to them.
Remember,
      Recite,
           Reminder,
Tonight.

"Stop thinking."

Dropping Petals

A bride walks down the aisle.
Step by step.
Little girls dropping petals
Drop by drop.
The bride feels her heart tighten up.
She averts her eyes from the children,
But she can still hear the petals:
Drop by drop.
Soon all shall be over
Her being is no longer her own
She belongs to her lover.
All that is left
Of this blushing bride—
A stem cut from its roots.
She has become
A rose unraveled.
She meets the eyes of her handsome groom
And in them, she sees the devil.
With a poison kiss
From his lips,

She released her fingers
From the last petal.

Veil

A mirage so hazy.
Yet not invisible to *your* eye.
With a white veil adorned around her head
It drapes across her hidden face.
Her dark, sweet enchanting gaze,
Boring, staring, searching yours.
So beautiful, that you cannot look away.
You'll pull the veil from her face
Before you are greeted with *it*...
The one you have tried so hard to suppress!
Until you hear *it* screaming in your head:
It's me, it's me!
Come see, see, see?
Your virgin bride wraps her petite fingers 'round your neck
And whispers:
Squeeze, squeeze, squeeze...
This horrible curse you've brought upon yourself

When you married the woman in the veil
Little, little did you know,
You have married a monster from Hell!

Luck

Here I lay sleeping in a bed like a cot.
My back is sore and my bones crackle and crunch,
Yet I'm only twenty-one.

I dream for a life of solemn divinity
Yet live such an uncomfortable one.
I hear cars honking,
Tunes blasting throughout both my ear drums.

The American dream now is an impossible one,
Only gifted from brushstrokes of dwindling luck.
Yet still, we dream, and dream and dream
For a life worth living,
One of meaning
To be our own saving grace.
But people like me barely have a chance
Of conquering such things.

Because those who say:
Follow your heart.
And succeed,
Were born under the eye of luck.

The ones who live and die happy
Are oh so few of us.

Time

How can someone run out of something that doesn't exist?
Time is predictable, of course
We know when the clock strikes twelve
Depending on the sun or the moon
It could be night,
Or it could be noon.
Three, Eleven, or Eight, you say—
But who decided the hours, the days?
Who do we follow blindly into the dark?
The one who chose to count Time is the one who feeds on us.
The one who watches us through curtain drapes,
We have become Time's slave
Ten, Two, Nine, or Six?
Beneath the surface, Time does not exist!
Time is a manipulation of uncurious thought.
Time, Time, Time is a ticking, ticking bomb

And we are ever aware.
And this truth holds such omens, it seems,
Not knowing the intervals of one's reality,
The Time on the clock will reach its meet
For all of us indeed.
How long will humanity count the time
Four, Seven, One, or Five?
Until it bleeds before our eyes.

The Dream

I dream of a man cloaked in grey.
Mysterious and strange, and I must say
That this man of which I dream is no man at all.
Not of this world.
He is a ghost from a past I'd rather forget
One I've grown to deeply regret.
I've distracted myself with mindless intent
To rid my mind of this man cloaked in grey
He comes to my dreams covered in a shroud
His eye bright, gleaming with flames.
In a dream of a dream where I dream of he,
These dreams wilt be the death of me.

Nightmare

I see visions of you
Inside my dreams.
And I am more hurt now,
Than it visibly seems.
Loving you was my single regret.
Now memories of you
Are all that is left.
I see your face in all my nightmares
This recurring dream I keep having of
you.
Keeps pulling, pulling, pulling me in two.
You haunt me now
Every waking day.
And the constant thought of you
Never goes away.

Demon

My lover was a demon.
He tainted my thoughts,
Clouded my mind with a haze of insanity
And I so believed that I was happy.
My lover was a demon,
He locked me away.
Fed me with absentminded love,
Yet I so believed he kept me safe.
My lover was a demon.
He found pleasure
In corrupting me, torturing me
Before he left me to die.
And when I gaze into the reflective glass,
Feeling ever so high
No longer do I recognize she;
For he remains in me.

Monster

Eyes contrast against the dark;
Glowing bright, iridescent.
Far, yet I can feel its careful breaths.
Vague whispers tickle my long, soft hair.
I see it in my nightmares, everywhere.
Soulless eyes,
Peer behind a gray polyester hood.
Fiery blue, staring intently.
Watching me.
Even after a year and three months, it
hasn't faded yet.
That monster is still inside my closet.

Lucifer

I wrack my brain, dissect my thoughts
I search each bloody crevice
And leave behind footprints of a
wandering soul
To find my confession buried deep inside;
Seared into my flesh like oak
Carved out of a withering tree.
No matter how I much wish, I cannot
confess these sins.
The poison I bled upon thine cross was
not mine!
I know that the Almighty cannot forgive
me,
For the sin that I hath done.
I fell for him and died for him.
The fallen, fallen, fallen one.
An embodiment of doubtless beauty,
And with a light inside him
Brighter than the burning torch.
He appeared to me an apparition
Of my wildest dreams and thoughts.

And now here, at my untimely end,
How dare I ask of His gracious hand to forgive me,
When his name in my brain will not resurface?
O! I feel a stinging surge of memory...
That's it! That's right!
Now I remember!
The name he had, the cursed name he bore
Was that of Lucifer.

How Will It End?

Oftentimes I find myself thinking about
Death.
And always, I ask myself: How will it end?
On a plane, in a crash?
From an animal attack?
May I die by my own hand?
Or maybe even drown in the face of
quicksand?
Will it be by a gun, a shot,
In the middle of a parking lot?
Oftentimes I find myself thinking about
Death.
How many times have I faced the
indefinite end?
Yet I do not have an inkling,
Forever and ever and ever unknowing.
How much longer do I have,
Before I, myself become one with Death?
Before my body is left an empty vessel.
Will I leave this world as someone
important?

Or will I forever be insignificant?
You see I am left at a loss,
I will never truly know the cause.
All of us, we must wait.
Until it has become far too late.
So, tell me, tell me, tell me please.
Relieve me now, my curiosity.
Oh death, oh death.
How will it end?
How will it end,
Oh Reaper of Death?

Insane

I am stuck here,
Bound in chains.
And this is where
I shall remain.
The thought of you
Inside my brain,
Is driving *me*
Quite insane?

Monologue of a Girl on Death Row:
A Lovely Death

I never intended for it to turn out this
way,
But lack of sleep could drive anyone crazy.
I don't know what I was thinking
When I took that first slash at his throat.
He awoke!
And looked at me, terrified
With frightened eyes.
I didn't stop, I couldn't!
I held on tight to the kitchen knife
And stabbed him,
Again and again.
He gripped his throat to stop the incessant
bleeding and reached to take the knife
from me.
But I wouldn't let go, I couldn't!
I held it so tight, my knuckles turned
white.
I felt something I never did before, a high!
When he stopped breathing

Wide open, his eyes!
In them I see myself,
My face stained with splashes of his blood,
and a sick maniacal grin plastered onto
my delicate features.
For the first time in my life…
I felt beautiful.

Since being in this prison cell,
Clad in orange,
Bound with a chain for a belt.
I haven't slept better!
The dream of me killing him replays
Over and over in my head.
The sound of his screaming; a lullaby
instead.

It's the sweetest nightmare—a lovely
death…

Buried Alive

Scoop, crumble.
The sounds of a shovel.
Scoop, crumble.
The sounds of a shovel.
I hear the sound of crumbling above.
Where is he? Where is my love?
My face is concealed with a mask of dirt.
Open my eyes as I sink into the earth.

I must be going straight to hell...
When skin breaks, blood seeps through.
To protect internally, to mend the wounds.
And in this moment, I can feel the blood of the earth.
Pulling me inside its watery stream of dirt.

My body is frozen, and I cannot escape.
It does not matter how hard I scrape—
My nails, my nails, they all break!

All this suffering, all in vain!
Maybe I'll feel better if I scream.
So, I open my mouth and try to breathe.
When suddenly, suddenly,
My throat clogs up with muggy soil.
And I have never felt worse turmoil.
I cannot breathe, I cannot breathe!
These huge muddy hands, they're crushing me!

The soil engulfs my body and sucks me inside.
Is this what it feels like to be buried alive?
Scoop, crumble…
The sounds of a shovel.
Scoop, crumble…
The sounds of a shovel.

X Marks the Spot

I know why it's called
"X marks the spot"
Not to find hidden riches buried away in a wooden chest,
With jewels and gold and bright white pearls.
X is where a treasure much deeper lie.
With strings and beats and air.
Yes, dear pirate, you understand it now.
X marks the spot
Where he punctured my heart.

Stabbed in the Back

A kiss of chapped, prickly lips
Whispers softly into my mind
A sharp pain hit,
And lingers inside.
Trails like rivers of trickling blood
Caress my spine.
I stare into his eyes
And then a crack, a break!

He pulls away from my embrace
A serrated knife within his grasp!
Dripping dark fluid, almost black.
As I tried to take in a breath,
I felt it again!
A break, a crack!

A pained moan escaped my lips
'Twas in the middle of my back
A break; a crack!
Have I been stabbed?
A break; a crack!

I have been stabbed.

Bullet

Shoot a broken bullet through my heart;
Bursting through veins with one last beat.
Watch the blood paint words I wish I
could say
Across the blank canvas of my vessel.

Claws

His claws dug into my flesh,
And ripped the stitches from my chest.
My blood, my love, he drained it all
Until there was nothing left.
A permanent mark—struck my heart.
His claws hath left the deepest scar.

Scars

Wounds always leave a scar, be it a
scratch or a gash.
You'll have no clue until it happens to you
And could never understand without
dirtying your hands
That invisible scars linger quite deeply
too.

Martyr

He struck you with words,
As your veins split apart
In that wretched organ, we call the heart.
He didn't feel it then
Or perhaps he did,
But not enough to be a Martyr like us.
But don't worry love,
Because soon he'll know
What it's like to be used,
Beaten, broken, and bruised.
No, love
Not by you and not *for* you.
Because you see,
He's already free.
No, he will never understand thee;
Until he becomes the martyr of a love
That he truly believes.

Grave Robber

A greedy man
Had a plan
To get the riches he desired.
He was a thief, a cheat, and hated to work.
So, in a search for jewels and rarity stones,
He unearthed my tomb.
The treasure was burrowed deep within
my flesh
So, he pulled me apart
Piece by piece.
My clothes were tattered;
Worn from decay,
His hands covered in red.
And when he found the diamond he was
looking for,
My casket knocked his head.
Swirling patterns of kaleidoscope dreams
Filled the roof of his eyes
And through them, he saw me! Well—
My rotting skeleton.
He panicked, frantic and tried to escape

My final resting place,
But the casket was sealed shut, you see…
And when the man who tends the graves
Discovered a hole in the ground,
He lifted the lid open to see
A thief with hands caked in red.
Frozen, out of breath, petrified, *dead*.

The Bartender

A man at the counter owns the bar.
Where he mixes flavors of customer's delight.
But he also has drinks from his own special stash
And after all festivities are done,
People return home from a night of fun
And he finds himself alone in his pub.
He picks up a bottle of what appears to be
Wine: ripe, and red!
But as he lifted the bottle to touch his lips,
The bitterness darkly licked his tongue
Flowing through his fangs.
The essence of this invigorated the man,
Filled him with familiar energy
The taste addicting to him like caffeine.
Who drinks coffee black, you may ask?
The same kind of man who'd drink the juice from a skull.
The scent is strange, sweet, enticing!

A young woman appeared inside his bar after hours.
Caught in the act, he smiled at her, and gave her a glass.
Complementary as desired.
She revealed to him her darkest thoughts,
Assuming he was a simple stranger.
But this bartender was no ordinary man
As he slashed at her neck with a shard of glass!
It spilled, and it bled, but he stopped it with a kiss.
His mouth darkened and tainted in red!

-SUICIDE-

Oh, Lovely Noose

Oh noose, oh noose,

Oh, lovely noose,

You hang so high in the dead of night,

Help the bride to see the light.

Oh noose, oh noose,

Please don't come loose.

Her heart lifts into the stars,

But she falls to hell with all her scars.

Oh noose, oh noose,

Oh, lovely noose,

The corpse swings slowly in the cold,

A single tear too much to hold.

Oh noose, oh noose,

Oh, lovely noose,

Oh noose, oh noose,

Please don't come loose…

Kiss Me, Zombie

Zombie, Zombie, come to me, lovely.
I've been waiting, waiting, waiting for you, Zombie.
Bite me, bite me, bite me slowly.
Addicted, addicted to the pain you cause me…
Infect me now with the deadliest toxicity,
And ravage my body with charming simplicity.
Tear out my flesh and contaminate—
The purest blood that flows throughout my veins!
A simple kiss is how it shall start,
Until it is time to tear out my heart.
So kiss me, kiss me, kiss me, Zombie.
Let us lose our minds in a feasting frenzy!
All those around think I've gone crazy.
But you're the one who knows me, truly.
So kill me, kill me, kill me, Zombie.
Lay me, lay me down to sleep.

In a satin lined casket, of passionate disease.

So that I may rest, and rest in peace…

Hickey

The warmth of his tongue against my neck
Indentations his teeth had left.
Salivated poison drained
The blood from my flesh.
Bruises left behind were stained
Soft pinky red.
Soon, it bled a purple tint
That lingered deeper than the skin.
The mark was laced with aged decay
That night, tonight, and every day,
It is visible on my neck
Even after it had cracked.
Broken fast from the impact
Of a foolish desperate plight, surreal.
It's still there, it never healed.
If you look closely at my broken body,
You can see it ever clearly
The last hickey he gave to me.

Floating Roses

Roses lie in a bath afloat
Away they go and 'round they flow
Against calm waves where a girl rest alone.
She basks in relaxation; surrounded by candles.
Dark hair pools beneath a teacup rose
That floats across her chest.
She reaches up to take the pretty rose in her hand…
But a pain shoots through her arm as she winces
And drops the rose back into the bath.
Down, down, down it sinks through clear soapy water,
The murky line of red;
A trail of blood that spilled from her hand.
The roses float closer, in clusters this time
Each wanting a taste of her blood.
She pushes them away,

Paled arms scrape against thorns and petals—razor sharp!
Screams turn to shrieks as she cries out in weeps,
And the roses only move closer.
Pulled petals surround her as she bleeds out
Until they float back into the calm waves
As her hands twitch with the last signs of life.
A gentle tear glistens against candlelight.

She's fallen into a sleep of early demise,
And the murderer floats away, free.
She sleeps with dreams of suicide,
And the murderer floats away, free.

Chandelier

Teardrop-shaped crystals dangle from
flickering candles.
Her eyes reflect,
Tears stream like rivers down her cheeks.
As the Chandelier breaks.

The Siren of the Wandering Sea

You were an explorer; a sailor in a boat.
When you found me out there all alone.
So, you provided me shelter—
A home out of water;
Taught me to see past the horizon line
And I believed you'd always be mine.
Until the perilous storm arrived
Swept me back into the sea,
Your boat, your boat, it had capsized
And with the ocean had taken me.
So, I wrote a message in a bottle:
When you come to look for me,
Swim away to the deepest sea.
The color of your eyes; the brightest blue,
That is where I will wait for you.

After years and years and years of waiting,
In the waves of the wandering sea.
I became a siren in the depths;
I never saw your face again.
Still, I will continue to wait

So, come to me; don't be afraid
Because this is where I will always be.
One day soon you will find me,
The siren of the wandering sea.

-ADDICTION-

Smoke

You used to be a cigarette break.
Then you became the smoke in my veins.
It never felt so good to suffocate,
In our imaginary world, so desolate.
I used you just to get high.
Never once thought it would all be a lie.
You used to be a cigarette break.
Then you became the smoke in my veins.
I never felt so at ease,
When I caught your scent in the windy breeze.
I drank you in like the sweetest poison.
And in my mind, I'd lost all reason.
You were the one who tainted me;
You were the one who ruined me.
You used to be a cigarette break.
Then you became the smoke in my veins

Just suffocate me, punish me for being so naive.

Torture me, burn me for wanting to believe
That you were it, you were it.
My break from reality.
But with every puff the darkness loomed closer,
And with every kiss, my life was over.
A breath of air never felt so fresh,
As the smoky flames that lick against my spoiled flesh.

Lost Innocence

The intent in his eyes were clear as crystals,
Yet my foolish ignorance reaped control of me.
He shot through my heart with bullets of words.
Placed scattered kisses upon my tongue—
A tip coated with pale poison.
He kept his tight grip on me
With chains and shackles on aching wings;
Invisible to my naked eyes.
His lips caressed my hollowed breath.
He cradled me—a broken bird
As I slowly slipped into the depths…
Robbed of my innocence,
And thrown into waves and waves of insanity.

Condemned

He emptied wine glasses the color of
blood in my heart;
And such sentiments of love had been left
behind
In this condemned soul of mine.

Psychopath

The man I love is a psychopath.
He touched me; he came too close
And now I cannot
Let him go.

He may be a psychopath,
But I love him so.
His charming smile,
The tilt of his lips.
The glint in his eye holds a hint
Of horror, craze, insanity
That stirs a fire deep within me!

The man I love is a psychopath.
Trapped in this maze
He holds me in his
Entrancing gaze.

Although I have been loyal to him,
I fear he may want me dead.

Because even my love can't quench his thirst—
His bloody rage.

The man I love,
He's a psychopath!

Venus and Mars

Composed of love and timeless beauty,
Pure, naïve, and simply sweet
Kisses like birthmarks across her cheeks.
She sat in her garden and counted petals,
When the sun was overcast by a shadow.
He descended to her through slivers of light.
A man she could hardly recognize;
His hands were black, charred with smoke—
Skin bruised; arms bled deep with cuts.
With a head hung low—a voice devoid of words.
Violent, wrathful passion consumed this man.
Auras bled through and his heart burnt too.
Mars harbored such raw sorrows within,
A kiss from Venus could not heal him.
Instead, his heart grew evermore darker.
With kindness in his words

And deception in his eyes,
He charmed her.
With every touch, he left bruises
Around her neck and wrists.
Venus hated to admit,
She really did love him.
This love she felt was loyal—pure,
But Mars was robbed of his.
So instead,
He shared with her
All his darkness.

Art Exhibit

Display us in a gallery
For strangers to observe.
Let us become a singular work
You and I—together.
Let parts of us be clear as day and others left unfinished
Like Michelangelo's mysterious figures from the Renaissance.
Let my lips tease and tilt in an all-knowing smirk
Like Da Vinci's "Mona Lisa".
Let the hue of our organs and rushing blood be a landscape of design—
Like Van Gogh's "Starry Night".
Limbs uneven and twisted with a tinge of blue
Like the phase of the infamous Picasso.

The love we shared was strong and vibrant
Like "The Scream" by Edvard Munch.

And in my dreams,
I hear *you* scream
My name as clear as stars.
Every kiss
Left upon my canvas
Riddled with streaks of scars.

Inside our own art exhibit,
We've been reduced to this.
An example, a lesson, just another statistic
Of why not to fall in love.

Will You Go to My Funeral?

Will you go to my funeral—
When I die?
I don't expect you to cry.
I don't expect anything—how could I?
For you to attend my funeral,
Want it should I?
When I die, when I die.

Buried in the grass.
That love has passed.
It's shattered in pieces like broken glass.
I knew. Yes, I knew!
It wouldn't last.
Yet… I never saw it coming,
It happened so fast.
When I pass, when I pass.

Murdered by a butchered heart.
You know it was you—
You who flayed it,
And sliced it and ripped it apart!

This broken heart, my broken heart.

Can I make one simple request?
To see your face before I pass?
Will you fulfill this dying wish, my dying wish?
Before we reach the end of this.

So, answer a question, please.
When all is said, and all is done.
Never, never will I ever
Find the one
The one, the one.
So, answer my question, understand it well.
And answer true, but never tell.

Will you go to my funeral, when I die?
To bid me, once more, a final goodbye?

Rotten Kiss

Caress his head; a rotting skeleton.
Use his blood to paint my lips
Red; dark like a poison kiss.
Pull the sharp spike from his heart of
decay,
And lose myself to this insanity.
O' dearest skull of my beloved,
I will keep thee
Close to me
And remember you every passing day
With bloody kisses and rotten decay.

Pomegranate Love

Sickly-sweet
Love that spills through the ridges of uneven teeth.
Juice flows through the cracks;
Swallowed seeds get stuck in my throat.
These seeds are seeds that poison me.
For six months of every year, I live in fog.
For six months of every year, Mother grieves her loss.
Pomegranate love is a deadly love;
One that is felt too strong.
He lured me in with Pomegranate Love
And to me, Persephone sung.

Tainted Kiss

I cried tears of crystal ice;
Jagged and cold like his heart.
When it seeped past my black-coated lashes,
Blood trailed from beneath the cut.
The cut that was born when I cried my first crystal
The red filter crossed over my eyes
And rendered me blind.

His tainted kiss bruised my lips;
And turned them black as coal.
They tremble
With chittering teeth
And a mouth purple and numb.

His tainted kiss poisoned my mind
It shakes with pulsing distress.
The grooves in which a fungus grows
Transformed me into this.

Affliction

She suffered from insomnia and
philophobia
Such a tired, lonely girl;
Devoid of attachment and absent affection.
Imbalance of heart and mind was her
affliction.

Toxin

In space, all that waits
Is suffocation.
In water, all we do
Is drown.
But what in the world
Does a poor girl do,
When he breathes the toxin of love
Into once pure lungs?

Film Noir

I see it through my eyes
In black and white.
Boy meets girl;
Tries to give her the world
But she hates herself.

He says, "Baby you're my beauty. I love you so."
And with her eyes bright and wide she says:
"I wanna be a star
In film noir,
But we were born too late;
We've all got broken hearts."
But now that haunting silver screen has his name in lights,
And she's struggling alone;
Every night.

This beauty falls asleep now
With once wide eyes shut tight.

Releasing an empty plastic tube.
She sleeps away her broken dreams
And hides inside darker memories.

An Ill Mind

She was alone and sad, and she wanted someone to love her.
And when she sees his face, she thinks:

Maybe
For a moment, he can save me
From this comfortability
Of being sad and solitary?

But deep down, she knows he can't
This loneliness brews deeper than can be felt.
Deeper than any hole that can be filled
No amount of devoted affection will fix the pain.
Because the problem is not one of a lonely heart,
But a mind; ill and vain.

Flower in a Cracked Shot Glass

She was a flower in a cracked shot glass;
Drowning and burning simultaneously.
Her petals scattered across the fizzing drink
Before a light was tossed inside.
She crackled and burned in boiling flame
And her petals still screamed out his name.
He didn't hear her though, over the noise and the lights.
Before she withered to dust and died.

Molotov Cocktail

But don't you see?
My blood is gasoline.
You've set my heart ablaze.
Through torn up jeans,
The crackling flickers
Coursed throughout my veins.
You threw a flaming glass at me
And burned away my dreams.

Abused

In the beginning, I sat on his lap,
Holding a pink heart-shaped tray of used cigarette butts,
The numbness if his smoke overwhelmed me,
As every puff led to nonsensical love.
He hit me that night, but apologized;
With a shiny diamond ring.
I taped my busted lip and bruised lids shut;
Blinded when he says he loves me.
He lost his temper this morning,
Punched a hole into the wall,
And terribly frightened me.
Despite this though, with shaking hands, pale,
I kissed blood-spots against his angry knuckles.
His tangled-up heartstrings
Formed a noose around my neck,
But I stayed with him

Because I thought he loved me
And when he decided I was all used up
He left.
I stood in my room all alone
And succumbed to the darkness within.

A Sad, Drunken Little Girl

They ask me, "Why do you keep crying, little girl?"
I say nothing and take another swig
My eyes red and straining
With lips, a gentle tremble.
The wine is the only thing keeping me company
In a mindless state of perilous sublimity.
The glass against my lips is not enough for thee
I know, deep in the dark, he still hates me!
I can see through blurry eyes and dizzy spells;
He talks about me to his friends:
"She's pitiful, broken, and weak."
And they take his words as gospel
Knowing absolutely *nothing* of me!
But such things as these, matter little to me
While in a state of perilous sublimity.

Because when a little girl like me is sad
and yearning,
No soul, nor living body can rescue her
From such a willing defeat;
And nothing can ever be done to ease
Her method of self-suffering.

Graffiti Love

His art of love painted me-
A blank canvas.
He was no artist, he could barely hold a brush
But he still managed to paint a masterpiece of love onto me.
My skin is tainted from his touch,
My lips still taste his tongue,
Even today years have passed,
But my eyes still cry over his absence.
I miss him so, I never let him go
That must be the reason I can't stop crying.
The tears rolled over my chin, against my breasts.
They rolled down between my legs
Down onto the concrete around my feet.
The love he painted across my body-
Washed away by organic rain,
Falling from my distorted gaze.
He painted his masterpiece onto me,

And now it's washed away.
All remnants left of him are gone from me,
But for some reason
My heart still aches.

Please, Tell Me You Hate Me

Please, tell me you hate me
Even if you don't.
Please, tell me you hate me
I can't stand thinking about you all night.
When you ignore me,
My thirst for you grows more and more,
But at the same time,
I feel you drifting away from me.
Is it real or imaginary?
"Am I losing him too?"
No, no not again!

Please, tell me you hate me
So I don't have to think so much.
Please, tell me you hate me
Before we get too close.
Please, tell me you hate me
So I can just fucking forget.

Please, tell me you hate me
I can't take much more of this.

I feel like I'm slipping off the precipice
Of infatuation or love, I haven't a clue;
But it's insanity, and it's killing me.
I know you don't mean to.

Please, tell me you hate me
Tell me I'm annoying, to leave you alone
Tell me you can't stand seeing my name
on your phone.

Please, tell me you hate me
Don't drag this on longer than it needs to be.
Please tell me you hate me
Because this feeling of being unwanted hurts more
Than anything I've ever felt before.

Please, tell me you hate me
Even if it's a lie.
Please, tell me you hate me
So my heart stops skipping beats for you.

Please, tell me you hate me.
Don't be like the others;
If you really do intend to break me.

"Please don't hate me...."
Just pretend like you do.
"Please don't hate me..."
Because I love you.

Rose-Colored Moments

Netted stockings and tattoos cover up the abuse,
Cigarette burns and self-harm scars
Leftover from him on me.
His passionate anger and lustful kisses;
A suicide pact written in blood on the sand.
He left bruises around my neck,
In the shape of his hand.
I've damaged my body now,
Possessing only the broken bones of a sad, wilted rose.
Burnt flesh, wrecked heartstrings,
deepened scars
Leftover from him on me
For all my future lovers to see…
But I still recall
All those rose-colored moments:
Fond memories of him hurting me.

Numb

Tingle, tingle,
Pins and needles.
He left, he ran,
I'm all alone…
Tingle, tingle,
Pins and needles.
A feeling familiar
Aching with glum
Tingle, tingle
Pins and needles.
Now my love
I feel quite numb.

-DEATH-

Once Upon a Time

Once upon a time,
I met Prince Charming.
And believed everything he said.
Until through his lies, I myself became
An offal, bloody mess
He regretted this, you see,
So, he laid my body down in a bed of
frozen roses,
To bring me back to life.
But so much time has passed since then.
And I still lay here, broken and dead.

Side of the Road

Alone, a girl sits on the side of the road
Where she reads a book of sorrow.
As she turns the page,
She catches a glimpse
Of an old woman weeping in sorrow.

Broken Bones

I shall forever lay here alone.
In the dark, in the cold,
As my soul slowly, slowly grows old.
And I think to myself, where can I go,
When all that's left of me is broken bones?

Skeleton

Hollow vacancy fills these gaps
Like dust into the Earth,
All flesh degrades.
Rose buds bloom and mask
The lingering scent of haggard decay.
The rain sprinkles kisses across her cheeks
Red—a trail through the rivers—
Drowned with a sound
Of tearing whimpers.

O' Dusty Grand Piano

I danced atop his grand piano;
Left a kiss upon his nose
His fingers played a familiar tune
A perfect harmony; I sang the notes.
His keys enchanted my tapping toes,
I became his faithful muse.

I lie upon this grand piano—
Dusty and worn with age.
My musician, my lover, the man of the hour
His tunes still resonate
Inside my lungs as I sing into the night
In this desolate, silent theatre.
His eyes sunk in,
And his skin wore thin,
Yet his creaking chin
Bleeds bright with laughter.

Decay

When he fell in love with me,
I locked myself away.
From then on, it's been easy—
All scars and wounds astray.
Now it strains to feel beating—
What was once benevolent gleaming.
Sweet words from his lips
Kissed my fingertips
And spread throughout my veins.
Black fungus grew around my heart;
Such rapid, blooming decay.

Bittersweet

Wilted broken crumbled and grey
My notes and roses wither away
I'm shattered in mind, soul, and heart.
My bones, they crack
And veins strain against the beats.
But I will still sing
Songs of bittersweet insanity.

Baby Doll

I have innocent, decrepit, glossy eyes
Of old dolls that have been stuffed away
In an attic that smells like cigarettes
Amid the dusty air of melancholy.

Dream Girl

He told me I was his dream girl
But I turned out to be a nightmare.
My bright doe eyes
Sent a chill down his spine
And the curve of my lips
Made him cower and hide

He let me be his dream girl,
I kissed him in his sleep.
But now I'm a bloody nightmare,
One that waits in his dreams.

We were an impossible dream, you see.
Because he got too close to me.
He lied to me through his teeth,
Kissed me softly on the cheek.
Now, in reality,
I cry;
I weep.
I haven't forgotten and I regret
Anything and everything we did.

But as I am; a nightmare now,
I still take up space in his mind.
He knows I am the one he sees
The girl of which he will always dream.

Temporary

It has always occurred to me how beauty
is temporary.
How could you find love based on a
waning concept like that?
Wait for the one who will love you,
While your body rots in a velvet lined
casket.
One who will visit you every single day
To leave roses and lilies upon your grave.
Wait for someone who will kiss the ghost
of your lips
One who will caress your protruding
cheeks.
Wait for someone who will stare into your
eyes
Sunken into sockets and eaten by flies,
Wait for someone who will still love you
For thousands of years after you died.
Wait for someone who will not be as
temporary
As the mirror of your cracking vanity.

I'm waiting for him to find me;
Because I am guilty
Of choosing who to love
Based on faceless beauty,
Which means I could never possibly find him on my own.
So, instead, I'll wait until by body withers to bone;
I'll wait beneath my lone tombstone.
I'll wait for him to find me, then.
Because I don't trust myself now:
Both Alive, and Dead.

Immortality

I will be a ghost through words.
When you pick up my books,
You will hear me in your head.
I will linger on eternally,
Infinitely.
Through pages and pages of scribbled stories.
You will not see me,
But I can see you.

I know you're sitting in your room,
library, my tomb, or cemetery.
I can see you because I am a ghost—
an immortal ghost!
And I am waiting, watching *you.*

This is the key they all search for
And call it eternal youth.
But the key is written here,
Between the lines
Immortality.

Seasons

I once felt alive when I was standing in
the sun.
Heat against my skin; a soft breezing
wind.
Things have changed so drastically now,
But somehow it feels right.
When the leaves start to crinkle,
I feel more alive.
When days become lesser and nights
begin to linger.
When trees burn orange and yellow
instead.
Autumn, for me, is the perfect sunset.
When the warm summer breeze becomes
a chilling gust,
It makes me warm and tingly inside.
My heart beats faster when winter arrives.
And my nippy nose reminds me that I am
still alive.
Until spring rolls around the corner
And dread returns.

My body begins to feel so worn
By the end, I am reduced to what I was before.
The roses bloom; trees come to life
And the sun is visible in the sky.
It's summer now with scorching heat and humidity
Reminds me the cold was all just a dream.
Only do I remember then
How it feels to be dead again.

Picture Frames

Hallway with decrepit wallpaper peeling
at the edge.
A woman's face follows you through,
Weeping softly too.
A fireplace burns in the living room,
With ghosts playing dusty keys on the
piano.
The face comes back
Alight in picture frames
And red satin lies in flames.
Through her pain and vanity,
She rapidly decayed.

Fabric Flower Heart

Fabric flowers hold sweet scents
Far longer than real ones do.
My heart is made from fabric flowers.
The love from it bleeds shallow vibrancy,
Paused in a moment of eternal bloom
It will never fade;
It will never wilt
Like love tainted in truth.
Fabric flowers hold sweet scents
And mask the bitter taste of strained heartstrings.
Fabric flower hearts never break
They never wither;
And never fade.
Because a heart built from fabric flowers
Brews deception and hatred at its core.
My fabric flower heart has never led me astray
Because something, once beating,
Has already decayed.

Nyctophile

There was a reason I was always drawn to darkness.
Because in darkness, there's no end.
It goes on forever.
In darkness you're invisible.
In darkness you're never alone,
In darkness there is clarity;
Sweet, sweet serenity.
In darkness lies… simplicity;
Darkness is infinity…

My Last Wish

Like the plaster skulls of Jericho.
Never, never let me grow old.
Strip the flesh and blood from my bones,
And encase what's left of me in flawless stone!
Master Sculptor capture my likeness.
Let my body beam softly in everlasting brightness!
Scalp my long black hair from my rotten corpse
And weave it onto the head of my new gracious cocoon.
Please, for the love of God, make sure it never comes loose.
Replace my broken eyes with those of a doll,
And give me the longest lashes of all!
Clad my body in a long black dress,
Keep my vessel alive in the most lavish finesse.
Give my smile the slightest grin,

And be sure that my presence remains haunted.
Display my lifeless doll inside a rectangular glass.
And let no one even a foot near that lass!
Place my taxidermy cat upon my lap,
And the bag of my kittens urn within my grasp.
Sit me down on a throne made of black crow's feathers.
And please make sure all pieces stay together.
Because Master Sculptor this letter is for you.
I write it in hopes that you won't see it soon.
And if there comes a time you are unable to sculpt my doll,
Leave the task to your next pupil.
I'm entrusting you now with my last wish.
Now go, go, GO!
You have a job to finish.

Blood

You know, don't you?
That she is dead.
... and her blood
Is on your hands.

About the Author:

LiAna Maria Rivera is an artist of various mediums namely: writing, drawing, and music.

Her purpose in life is to call the inner melancholy that lay dormant within her and transform it into something beautiful in any creative way her mind wills it.

Her writing and art styles are heavily inspired by the romantic era of art and literature. As expected, she loves writing poetry, horror, and psychological thrillers. Despite this, she's a softie for beautiful love stories and likes to incorporate themes of love into a vast majority of her work.

She loves animals, but no animal more than Mr. BooBooKitty Cuddles, a black and white seven year young cat. Rainy, cloudy days spent cuddling with him and getting lost in a book are what happy times are made of for this strange lady.

When she's not cooing over how adorable her cat is, she's probably writing a blog post about how the decomposition process makes flowers shine brighter than the Supermoon.

HYSTERIA: A COLLECTION OF SHIVERS copyright © 2020 by LiAna Maria Rivera. No part of this book may be used or reproduced in any manner without written permission except in the case of reprints in the context of reviews.

ISBN: 9781951417048

Library of Congress Control Number: 2020902732

Cover Design and Illustrations by LiAna Maria Rivera

www.ingramcontent.com/pod-product-compliance
Lightning Source LLC
Chambersburg PA
CBHW030334100526
44592CB00010B/694